Sparks of Light Fly

poems by

Maria Elena Scott

Finishing Line Press
Georgetown, Kentucky

Sparks of Light Fly

Copyright © 2023 by Maria Elena Scott
ISBN 979-8-88838-177-9 First Edition
All rights reserved under International and Pan-American Copyright Conventions. No part of this book may be reproduced in any manner whatsoever without written permission from the publisher, except in the case of brief quotations embodied in critical articles and reviews.

ACKNOWLEDGMENTS

Great: Poems of Resistance, Fortitude and Subversion dedicated to November 9, 2016. January 2017, Edge of Grief

Love Letter To My Brother Juan: A Memoir In Prose, Poems and Found Text February 2022, A Family Nontheless, Ode To a Mexican Morning Glory, Tropical Bloom

Riverwest Currents, September 2021, A Dusting of Snow on the Chrysanthemum

Yellow Medicine Review: A Journal of Indigenous Literature, Art and Thought, Fall 2019, How I Learned To Make Gorditas

Publisher: Leah Huete de Maines
Editor: Christen Kincaid
Cover Art: CC0 Public Domain
Author Photo: Nick Scott
Cover Design: Elizabeth Maines McCleavy

Order online: www.finishinglinepress.com
also available on amazon.com

Author inquiries and mail orders:
Finishing Line Press
PO Box 1626
Georgetown, Kentucky 40324
USA

Table of Contents

Haiku # 1 1
Edge of Grief 2
Lingering Moment 3
There Is a Forever Place 4
Orphaned At the Border 5
Mexican Love Letter (For My Students) 7
Sister Ocean and Me (The Pacific at Lincoln City, Oregon) 8
When Lupe Got Her Voice Back 9
A Family Nonetheless 10
How I Learned To Make Gorditas 11
Ode To a Mexican Morning Glory 12
Tropical Bloom 13
Enduring Fear, Enduring Loss 14
Celestial Longing 16
Marking Time Long Ago 17
Fragments 19
For All Of Us: Helpless Bystanders At the Corner Of Cup Foods 20
Another One Felled 21
Sister Ocean and Me (The Atlantic at Virginia Beach) 22
What Comfort Girls Want Now That They Are Elder Adults 23
What Comfort Girls Want Now That They Are Elder Adults (Addendum) 25
A Dusting Of Snow On the Chrysanthemum 26
My Mexican Adonis (For Cesar E. Chavez) 27
Fragile Beings Sacrificed 29
Haiku #2 30

Haiku #1

Opaque clouds rush in
Your inner beauty obscured
Until you take flight

Edge of Grief (After the Election)

I know
I've been here before

The cold edge of grief is not new
I have lived here before

Melancholia 1 meets La Virgen de Guadalupe
Striding in tennis shoes

I know
    history
        has been
            here before

How will we respond this time?

Words wake up in me
They stop standing still

Punch through the ongoing nightmare

And silence?
Is not an option

Lingering Moment

Nestled in each other's curves
Our eyes closed
We surrender

Right here right now
My right hand holds your left

Where shall we go?

Like leaf fall
We sail where we will
Seeing ourselves there

There is a Forever Place
(The Gulf of México-Lauro Villar Beach)

Sonorous roaring sounds
soothe and scare

Aquamarine diamonds
play "hide and seek"

Mesmerizing foam
invites you to be baptized

We bathed in wind and sun

Held hands, a human chain of many

Tiptoed to Sister Ocean's embrace

Bobbed up and down screamed

buoyed by the next lapping wave

Swallowed gulps of sea

There is a forever place

Amazing life forms abound
sea stars oddly shaped clear jellies

No two-alike shells surrender
to the warm eroding wind

Sun-glistened water drapes
thirsty sand

We lost ourselves
 in months of endless wonder

A forever place
when everything held magic

Orphaned At the Border

Once upon a time, we walked in color.
We prayed:
Nuestra Señora de Guadalupe
Virgen morena give us peace, guide us.
Sang songs of hope and giving thanks

Now we just exist in black and white

We heard rumors about it
la hielera-the cooler cell.

We are all in cages here.
We do get a blanket each.
The blankets are like tin foil.
The cold floor is grey cement.

We have so many questions:
¿Hásta cuándo? How much longer?

No one knows the answer.

When will we see mamá?
When will we see papá?

Some of us have stopped crying.
Others just stare off into space.

When will we hug mamá?
When will we hug papá?

No one knows the answer.

¿Y de los bebés?
They go to sleep crying.
They wake up crying just the same.

Once upon a time we walked hand in hand.
We prayed together
We sang songs

Now we just exist in black and white

Mexican Love Letter
(For My Students)

I hold my people
Ruby red rebozo, embossed
La Catrina in a wide brimmed flowered hat. Honor Life!

I embrace my people
Festive multi-colored embroidered wrap, forehead to the sun
Bertha, Xochilt, Amada, Bernardo Jr. , Chilo, Maria, Lupita, Lily.
Celebrate life!

I mourn with my people
Pitch-black hearts, beaded on see through scarf
La muerte—death remembered

Dualities of life and death

I carry my people
Black and white cotton shawl, wide ample shoulders
Hope remained in the vessel. "I've got you…"

I give voice to my people
Fanned ribbons of shimmering wings
Tu historia es poder—Your history is powerful

—Sí, se puede, Sí, se puede… choral chants echo
We marched with the banner depicting La Guadalupana-Our Lady of Guadalupe, the patron saint of Mexico. Another person carried the familiar red background with an Aztec black eagle right in the center. Cesar Chavez and Dolores Huerta from UFW (United Farm Workers) led the charge from Delano to the capitol in Sacramento. Allies, Bobby Kennedy: hunger strikes, Treaty of Guadalupe, Bracero Program, Zoot Suit Riots, Walk Outs, Boycotts

I wrap myself in the fabric of all my people and those who love my Mexicanness!

Sister Ocean and Me
      (The Pacific at Lincoln City, Oregon)

As you lap at my naked, warm feet
Your clear cold invigorates

I start
One foot up—one foot down

Move closer

One foot up—one foot down

As you recede, I splash over and over again
Your next tickling wave
Roars excitement

I scream with glee:
"Here it comes.
Diane, hurry! Here it comes. Here it is. Yeah!"

Cool white foam caresses my ankles
One foot up—one foot down

I move closer

One foot up—one foot down

You lap at my feet
I dance wild

You tickle my soul
I scream for joy

Sister Ocean rhythms and me

When Lupe Got Her Voice Back

Lupe had withstood multiple stab wounds
Her jealous ex-boyfriend, the perpetrator
Injured both Lupe and their baby

Sutured cuts dot the right side of her pale face
And flicker at the light of the cameras
A gash to her neck is bandaged
From her right ear to the front of her left shoulder

Now home from the hospital
Surrounded by the puffed cushions of a comfy, crushed velvet chair

Lupe recounts "At first I thought he was (just) punching me
But then I felt the trickling blood."

The young mother warns those who are still silent:
"As soon as it happens, get out immediately!"

She cautions those who are in denial:
"With me it started just verbal. Don't let them control you!"

Lupe gingerly moves her arms up to a semi circle
She utters her daughter's first word
The word that her now dead six month old was learning to say to her
"Momma?" Lupe lets her arms rest on her lap

The smothering hold of sh-sh-sh, and don't tell
Was before and not any more

And while the television interview continues
Lupe lifts a sharp chisel with her left hand
A heavy mallet with her right

She swiftly shatters one metal link at a time
Sound waves flutter
Sparks of light fly.

A Family Nonetheless

We were ones without una mamá o un papá
Bound by unknown circumstances

We lived at La Guardería de Niños
An entire block-size space
Chain link fence on three sides
Grey cinder block framed the fourth wall of the orphanage

Leftover dollops of cement on the very top
Held spiky shards of broken bottled glass
Jade green. Amber brown. Some see thru clear. All jutted straight up

Rhythms rang our daily chores
Weekly rituals danced color and pageantry

The Augustine sisters taught all there was to learn
Of religion and behaving
We were a non-traditional family
A family nonetheless

Mamá Earth taught all there was to know and discover
Of seasons among the orchard
Los ciclos de limones, limas, guayabas, and morning glories for our senses

I was happiest when I knew my brother Juan was near
A family of two, then a family of three with José Reyes
A family of more than us

A pied piper with younger children always tagging along
I'd carry one on my left hip while another held on to my right hand
A family of many unrelated by blood

Bound by unknown circumstances

A family nonetheless

How I Learned to Make Gorditas

Strong brown hands
Knead, turn, knead and turn, fold and shape
An oddly shaped block of corn masa-dough

The cook at the orphanage taught me
How making tortillas and gorditas
Was daily, needed food

Not tall enough to reach the front burner
Of the small white stove
I stood on a wooden step-up
Kept near the locked pantry

Strong brown hands
Knead, turn, knead and turn, fold and shape.

"Take a small dollop of masa with your right hand
Put in your cupped left hand
Do not drop
Roll between both hands
When you have a just right orb shape
Pat the masa to flatten, about the size of the palm of your hand."

"Smooth the edges: like this
Now, carefully place it on the hot griddle."

Repeat.

Small brown hands obey.

Ode To a Mexican Morning Glory

I remember waking up at dawn
In Matamoros, Mexico

Sleepwalker
To a mural of stars
Against green wet vines

Behind the girl's dormitory

Dewdrop jewels glisten
On a carpet of sleeping grass

My bare feet moist as I reach
For a single just-right
Creamy white morning glory

A gentle caress
A soft pull
Lips taste, savor
Pliant flower food

Communion before daybreak

I remember the imprint of pollen
Formed freckles on my nose
Oh, how that golden dust made me feel

Tall, weightless, limber
Loved
For an hour or two

Or until the magic powder
Had gently sifted to my toes
And all I could do was
Await the dawn

Tropical Bloom

Before a Hibiscus flower falls

She knows the expectation
Rehearsed
Ancient memory

Wills the opening rhythm
awake unfurls
gauze red blooms

Over a span of time passing

Before a hibiscus flower falls

She tells herself: "Divert life energy
transfer nutrients
to nearby
closed blooms,
nudge and inspire."

Months of full color soften
Sunrays and dewdrops soothe

Before a hibiscus flower falls

She learns restraint
pulls back folds into herself
over weeks and days passing

Holds sun drenched
intoxicating breath…

Ahhhh, exhales   plum purple petal drops

Enduring Fear, Enduring Loss

What kind of morning is it when
You kiss your loved one off to work
Amid the smell of café and maple syrup
Again brushing away the doubt of your return?

What kind of noon time is it when
With a telenovela drama blaring on Telemundo
Caldo de pollo on the stove
Your heart sinks at the thought of Luisito's life without you?

What kind of dinner-time is it when
With anxious eyes I watch the glint of the front door knob
Sit down at the borrowed oak table
Por favor, God! Let it not be today a raid happens where he works

Your cold dinner plate sits empty, waiting

What kind of night-time is it when as you get ready for bed, you wonder
Why the mailbox did not hold that official looking envelope
Promised by the last immigration lawyer?

What kind of Tuesday morning is it, when in a haze you remember that
The echo of your work boots did not make it home
The "You are home!" ritual to calm your nerves neither?

Your cold dinner plate sits empty, waiting

Wednesday dinner time, waiting, Thursday dinner time, waiting
Four nights waiting, six nights waiting, eight weeks, ten weeks, waiting
twelve months

What kind of sunrise is it when the cold angst of another January
The limbo of another August
witness my tossing and turning, unable to sleep?
Our son, Luisito still wonders
What happened?
Why mamá?

Celestial Longing

As if in a ballet dream
I walked in the dark
To the fence post heading east

Raised my face up
To the sky
As far as my chin could arch

Stood silent in prayer
Vapor painted
Tiara circles around you
Luminous Snow Moon-Luna Nevada y brillante
I placed a small potted plant to rest
On my right shoulder

A winterberry offering
Overflowing
Succulent
orb clusters
Candy cane red

Snow Moon-Luna Nevada y brillante
Longing to kiss this sphere where I am
Firmly planted

You've (spun 'round your own axis)
rotated close
Closer, closest
This night proximity is on our side

Do you see: white caps of snow on peaks?
Three quarters of me liquid blue?
Shades of brown beneath the whirling mists?

I am Earth!
Your forever lover

Marking Time Long Ago

Birthdays in Mexico...
no cake
no candles
no Pin the Tail On the Donkey games

Not celebrated at La Guarderia de Niños orphanage in Matamoros, Mexico

Yearly celebrations
Pageantry
Yes, of course!
Fiestas de guardar—days of obligation?
Yes. Celebrated.

Buñuelos after midnight mass
hundreds of them
palm sized, flour dough orbs
stretched out, rolled to flat, lightly fried
crisp, cinnamon-sugar laden pastry,
crystal freckles lingered on my face and hands

Milagros and votive candles lit
Constant pleas for miracles

Weekly rituals:

Mass?
Latin orations and incense
When to stand up, kneel or sit?
Just follow the elders' lead

Confession?
A menu of sins rotated
White tissue paper doves
Gifts of beauty and hope

Communion?
Memorize the catechism first
Open your mouth, receive the holy host on your tongue
Beware it may stick
to the roof of your mouth

I did receive birthday presents in Mexico
however oddly marked by the rituals
of a different calendar

Fragments

I wonder

Does my image
Pop into someone else's mind
The way it happens in mine?

Out of the blue

While

Placing a bowl in the kitchen sink
Walking outside to get the day's mail
Closing a magazine in bed?

A split second occurrence

That certain lover, colleague, friend
From before and long ago

Whose name I may have forgotten
But whose story I still remember?

Did they find their way back home?
Did she move to San Diego like she'd planned?
Is he still living in Madison?

I wonder
Does my image
Pop into someone else's mind like that?

For All Of Us: Helpless Bystanders Outside Of Cup Foods

"When can you kill another?
When what's inside of you is already dead." *

Brave under age witness turns on her smart phone and records
A Black man terrified, struggling to breathe
With the full weight of a cop kneeling on his neck!

He was trying to gasp for air
Suffering
He was trying to move his head to get air
Moaning in pain
He cried for his mother

The cop taunted him:
Get in the van then!
I will. I can't breathe!

Two other officers were holding him down
He was saying how much in pain he was
They wouldn't let us get close.
They put their hands on the mace
I didn't understand why the mace was needed

Were you an unruly mob?

I heard them say he can't breathe
His nose is bleeding
I heard them say get off of him
I heard them say he stop breathing
Check the pulse, man

"When can you kill another?
When what's inside of you is already dead." *

*A quote from the novel "Blindness" by José Saramango. Winner of the Nobel Prize for Literature in 1998

Another One Felled

I watched you grow for two complete
Rotations around the sun

From cool canopy silhouettes on the asphalt
To streaks of carotene quaking in the wind
From the coldest winter on record, you encased in ice
To the floods that introduced us to the neighbors
From chlorophyll fed buds
To your full-fledged opened, glossed newness

Fluorescent orange circle marked
You were next to be cut down, not that one over there, but you
You, whose face I had grown accustomed to observing daily

On a bright summer morning, on the corner of Burrell and
Montana Street
I sat witness on the front steps
Too late to save you, though I had tried

When I asked why, Beautiful One
Public forestry worker replied:

"That maple? Strangled itself
When it was planted, it was put in wrong."

Young sapling
You grew
Tightly bound
Like a baby girl's feet tightly wrapped in the China of long ago

Knowing that your roots could not spread out to live long
I'm sorry Beautiful One
They didn't know how to free your rootball
Before planting you

Back then

Sister Ocean and Me
        (The Atlantic at Virginia Beach)

With feet firmly planted
Edge of foam and sand

I caress your horizon
Your sing song white capped waves

I wait exhilarated
Ancient rhythm known for ages

Ballet step closer
Touch your bubbling excitement

Trickster Wind whips my long (mostly black) hair this way and that
Tickles my happy sun drenched face

Laughing aloud I move wisps of hair out of my mouth
Step back, watch my footprints erase

You splash tag me! Whoa!
I don't fall, only wobble and scream for joy

I am your beloved dancer
You are my forever romance.

What Comfort Girls Want Now That They Are Elder Survivors

When I was thirteen years old, armed soldiers came to our village.

It was a very bad time for us then
They beat up my father bad
So he could not do anything to save me
He could not even say "Stop."
They had a gun pointed at his head.

Today I want to be someone's
Precious daughter
Someone's
Precious niece
Precious friend

My father loved me
I know this because
He used to call me over
And feed me
White rice
Not sorghum
White rice
My mother would get mad at him for this
That's how I know he loved me

The armed soldiers
Just took me away from my house
Took away a friend
And two other girls

For years after the war
We held our shame in
For something
We.did.not.even.want
This happened at a
Comfort Station

(Another woman speaks tentatively.)

I want to remove
this thorn in my heart
I will tell the truth
This thorn
I will tell my children
In my heart I want to be where
The other comfort women are protesting.

I think I can		then tell the truth
of what happened		when I was kidnapped
and beaten		and raped all of the time."

(At the protest rally)

"We have our voices now!
We want an apology!
We will burn away the shame in us!
That rests with you, Japan!
With YOU!"

When I was thirteen years old, armed soldiers came to our village.

What Comfort Girls Want Now That They Are Elder Adults (Addendum)

In 2001 Prime Minister Junichiro Koizumi wrote a letter of apology to the comfort women. Here is the translated letter:

"As Prime Minister of Japan, I thus extend anew my most sincere apologies and remorse to all the women who underwent immeasurable and painful experiences and suffered incurable physical and psychological wounds as comfort women. We must not evade the weight of the past, nor should we evade our responsibilities for the future.

I believe that our country, painfully aware of its moral responsibilities, with feelings of apology and remorse, should face up squarely to its past history and accurately convey it to future generations.

Furthermore, Japan also should take an active part in dealing with violence and other forms of injustice to the honor and dignity of women.

Finally, I pray from the bottom of my heart that each of you will find peace for the rest of your lives.
Respectfully yours,
Junichiro Koizumi
Prime Minister of Japan

October 18, 2013 Prime Minister Shinzō Abe: " The Abe Cabinet will take the same stance as that of past Cabinets."

A Dusting of Snow on the Chrysanthemum

Summer to autumn season dawns

Groupings of wine red colors
Arrays of burned sienna abound

Large and small planters
Brimming full of cheery mustard yellows

You do want to extend the life of your garden, no?
Chrysanthemums are the easiest flowering annual to grow

One last hurray before the cooling breezes invite
Old Man winter to the dance

All the places with garden centers have them
Lowe's and Menard's even grocery stores

Have you cleared a spot to plant them in your garden?
Will you arrange them in containers on the front porch?

The sheer number of domed flowers in one pot
Is enough to make me swoon

Cone shaped petals smallest in the center
followed by the next size larger and so on

Faint talcum powder perfume with tones of spices
From the fabled orient permeate the air

The blooms stay fresh for days
The dusting of faerie magic freeze dry the bunch

Fully opened
Facing sun beams

Light refracts on the chrysanthemum

My Mexican Odonis
    For Cesar E. Chavez

Sunlight kissed
Melanin bronzed

Smile lines illuminate your kind eyes
Mother Earth furrowed; seeds planted

Campesino among campesinos

Calloused hands tilled, pruned and harvested fruit
Up down ladders without water to drink

Paid at the whim of the growers, a few cents per load
On to the next crop: you tilled, weeded and picked vegetables

Without a break in dangerous temperatures
Toxic pesticides rained on you. Inanimate object to the sprayers

_!Huelga-Strike! Boycott grapes!
_!Con la union se vive major! Life will be better when we unionize!

You carried us, all of us, on ample shoulders; brown Adonis with your love.
We learned to stand together for justice and hold our heads up high.

_Si, se puede chants were our chorus pilgrimage
From Delano all the way to Sacramento

You starved for us, all of us, brown Adonis as a prayer
.
They say you died in your sleep
I say you died from pesticides and the hard labor of multiple harvests.

They say you went to bed late, fell asleep and just didn't wake up.
I say your body shut down from the stress of non-violent resistance

I honor you today
Many decades later and behold:

Your Smile lines
Mexican Adonis

Mother Earth furrowed
Seeds planted

Fragile Beings Sacrificed

U. S. soldier broken
Monarch butterfly on the brink

Fragile Beings
need safe corridors to travel.

There is light from the east.

Lost Beings
need dependable guideposts to find their way back.

There is light from the north.

Delicate Beings
need specific nutrients to make them strong.

There is light from the west.

Tenuous Beings
need the gift of time to emerge.

There is light from the south.

Frail Beings
need to be known in the context of their past.

In all directions

Light
Transforms.

Haiku # 2

Salmon colored blooms
Look! How beautiful you are
Fully facing light

Maria Elena Tormey Scott is a Mexican American, bilingual writer and poet. A graduate of U.W. Madison in Education. Former bilingual educator for 25 years. Invited poet at the following events in Milwaukee, Wisconsin.

She was invited to read her poetry at the following venues/events before moving to Richmond, Virginia:

Alice's Garden 09/07/2017
Poets Read Some Stuff Somewhere In Milwaukee 09/14/2017
The American Dream: Art For and By Immigrants 07/21/2017
The Earth Poets and Musicians 30th Annual Performances 04/21/2017
35 Days of Don't: Celebrating Defiance and Bodily Autonomy 03/18/2017

www.ingramcontent.com/pod-product-compliance
Lightning Source LLC
Chambersburg PA
CBHW022126090426
42743CB00008B/1029